PREACHING CHRIST

Edgar Andrews

ET Perspectives No 1

Published by
EVANGELICAL TIMES
Faverdale North, Darlington, DL3 0PH, England

E-mail: theeditors@evangelicaltimes.org

Web: http://www.evangelicaltimes.org

First published June 2005

British Library Cataloguing in Publication Data available

ISBN 0-9500129-1-2

Printed in Great Britain by Athenaeum Press, Gateshead, UK

PREACHING CHRIST

CONTENTS

page

Publisher's Note

The chapters of this booklet first appeared as a series of articles in *Evangelical Times* during 2004, though Chapter 7 has been added since. In response to requests, these articles now appear in collected form — as the first of what we hope will be a series of booklets under the generic title *ET Perspectives*.

From time to time, *Evangelical Times*, a monthly newspaper, publishes series of articles on a variety of subjects, ranging from historical to theological, from practical Christian living to Bible exposition. The Editors feel that these series are often of sufficient interest to warrant being made available in their own right, and have therefore launched *ET Perspectives* as a means to this end. Each such series is normally of a length that lends itself to reprinting as a booklet — hence the present (and hopefully future) publications.

Our prayerful hope is that these inexpensive booklets will be of use in furthering the gospel of the glory of our Lord Jesus Christ and bringing men and women to a deeper knowledge of his unsearchable riches.

The Editors
Evangelical Times

Author's Preface

I preached my first sermon about fifty years ago and have learned a lot since then! However, one thing has not changed — my conviction that the only preaching that really counts is that which centres on the Person, work and glory of Jesus Christ, the eternal Son of God.

My preferred method is to preach consecutively through a book or section of the Bible, and this inevitably means dealing with many different issues in the course of a series of sermons. Such preaching moves constantly to and fro, from the mountain peaks of God's eternal purposes to the valleys of practical experience, spiritual conflict and perplexity. But I have never found a passage in the whole Bible that does not point in some way to Christ, the Lord of glory of whom those scriptures testify.

Today, however, much evangelical preaching lacks a consistent Christological dimension and churches languish as a result. In the 1950s the church I then attended was experiencing a season of great blessing, with many young people (especially young men) being saved under the ministry of Pastor Ian Tait. The minister of a nearby church asked him what was the secret of this success. 'I think', he replied, 'that whereas you say, "Come to church", we say "Come to Christ".' He was right. Even in these days when few are being converted, believers are blessed and built up by Christ-centred preaching and teaching. Even more important, such preaching glorifies Christ and pleases God the Father (2 Corinthians 2:14-15).

This is something we need to rediscover. Some preachers may even need convincing that Christ-centred preaching really is the biblical way. Others accept the principle but find the practice hard to follow. This small booklet is offered with a genuine desire to help such people, as well as to encourage those who strive with Paul 'to preach ... the unsearchable riches of Christ'.

Finally, I ought perhaps to apologise for the fact that the title of this booklet is the same as that of a similar length publication from the Banner of Truth Trust, namely, their 2003 reprint of Charles McIlvaine's 1863 address entitled *Preaching Christ*. Given the subject matter of the present booklet, this was unavoidable. However, I warmly commend the Banner publication to the reader for, although my approach is quite different, my message is precisely the same. I believe the reader will benefit from reading both.

Edgar Andrews
Welwyn Garden City, Hertfordshire, UK
April 2005

1. WHAT SHALL WE PREACH?

'For we do not preach ourselves,
but Christ Jesus the Lord,
and ourselves your servants for Jesus' sake'
(2 Corinthians 4:5).

I doubt whether anyone called to preach would quarrel with the apostle Paul's sentiments. In theory at least, we all agree that Christ is to be preached.

But experience shows that good intentions are not always carried out. Preaching some time ago at a church whose pastor had recently retired, I later received a note of thanks. It said that out of the dozen or so visiting preachers who had served the church, only two of us had preached a Christ-centred message.

One suspects this is a common experience. Further indications that all is not well come from books, conferences and articles on preaching. Many of these contain little direct reference to preaching Christ (there are honourable exceptions, of course).

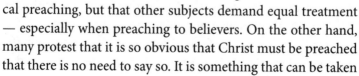

We read about expository preaching, relevant preaching, preaching with power, preparation for preaching, and so much else, but somehow the content of the preaching often seems to be forgotten. There are two main reasons for this. Some genuinely feel that Christ should not be the sole focus of evangelical preaching, but that other subjects demand equal treatment — especially when preaching to believers. On the other hand, many protest that it is so obvious that Christ must be preached that there is no need to say so. It is something that can be taken for granted. However, in practice, the result is often the same — a failure to preach Christ. The purpose of this booklet is to explore what it really means to preach Christ and why it is essential to do so.

Some statistics

Let us begin with some approximate statistics — culled from Young's analytical concordance (and thus based on the King James Version). The words 'preach' or 'preaching' in our English New Testament are used to translate as many as eleven different Greek words (some of them closely related). However, the majority of references to preaching involve just three Greek words, meaning respectively: to evangelise or tell good news (49 times); to herald or proclaim (61 times); and to tell thoroughly (10 times).

I shall refer to this again in the chapters that follow, but more significant for our immediate purpose is the subject or content of New Testament preaching. Of the around 132 uses of the English verb 'preach' in the New Testament, the following can be said. In 39 cases the word is used generally, without identifying any specific content (except in the case of John the Baptist's preaching of repentance, which is included in this figure). In one case, the subject of preaching is 'the faith'. In 12 cases, the subject is 'the word'. In 14 cases it is 'the kingdom' that is preached.

But a massive 67 references speak of preaching either 'the gospel' or 'Christ (or Jesus)'. Since the gospel is necessarily 'the gospel of the glory of Christ' (2 Corinthians 4:4), all these instances speak of preaching Christ. Furthermore, 'the faith', 'the word' and 'the kingdom' must all relate in some way to Christ, for he is the object of our faith, the subject of the word, and the ruler of the kingdom! It is no exaggeration, therefore, to say that whenever the New Testament identifies the subject of preaching, that subject is found to be Christ.

Implications and objections

This has important implications. It means that only Christ-centred preaching has New Testament authority. If we fail to proclaim Christ in our preaching we are robbing God of his glory and our hearers of their spiritual food. Could it be that even in evangelical churches today, 'The hungry sheep look up and are not fed'?

But some will raise objections at this point. For one thing, they will say, I have ignored the Old Testament, which is just as much the word of God as the New. This is a valid point and I intend to deal with it more fully in a subsequent chapter. But for the moment let me simply quote two Scriptures. The first is Jesus' statement to his critics: 'You search the [Old Testament] Scriptures, for in them you think you have eternal life; and these are they which testify of me' (John 5:39). The second relates what happened on the Emmaus road, when Jesus chided the two downcast disciples for their slowness 'to believe in *all* that the prophets have spoken!' Then 'beginning at Moses and *all* the prophets he expounded to them in *all* the Scriptures the things concerning himself' (Luke 24:27; note my added emphasis).

These Scriptures do not prove that the Old Testament contains nothing but Christ-related material, but they do put us on notice that Christ himself regarded the Old Testament Scriptures as a massive and concerted testimony to himself. Clearly, then, we *may* preach Christ from the Old Testament just as truly as from the New. I would go further to say that we *must* do so, but the case for this will be developed as we proceed.

Only for the unsaved?

A second objection is that while we should preach Christ to the unconverted, this is no longer a priority for the believer. There are many other things to engage the attention of the converted soul, we are told. A much-quoted example is Samuel Bolton's aphorism: 'The law sends us to the gospel that we might be justified; and the gospel sends us to the law again to enquire what is our duty as those who are justified' (The true bounds of Christian freedom, 1645).

This implies that while we must preach the gospel to the unsaved, we should make the law our priority in preaching to Christians. I disagree profoundly, but this is not the place to debate the role of the law in the Christian life — I am here just illustrating the contention that some regard 'preaching Christ' as a ministry to the unsaved rather than the saved.

This is a large and often confused subject, and again a full treatment is postponed till later. But let me offer a brief reply to this objection here. Where does the epistle to the Hebrews bid Christians look as we 'run the race that is set before us'? Is it not 'to Jesus, the author and finisher of our faith' (Hebrews 12:1-2)? It is indeed. For Christ is not only the author of our faith — he is the only one who can bring it to perfection and completion! If that is so, to take our eyes off him — for whatever reason — is perilous. This surely is the whole burden of Hebrews. And it follows that those who preach to believers must surely preach Christ, so that they might be able to 'consider him' (Hebrews 12:3) —meaning study him, ponder him, concentrate on him, and give him our full attention.

A sweet savour of Christ

Let me conclude this chapter by pointing out what is accomplished when we preach Christ. When Paul comes to Troas 'to preach Christ's gospel', he sees his preaching as something that 'diffuses the fragrance of [Christ's] knowledge in every place'. This is true whether the hearers receive his message and are saved or reject it and perish (2 Corinthians 2:12-15). Moreover, this fragrance of the knowledge of Christ is not only diffused among men but also rises 'to God' — like incense offered on the altar in the tabernacle. That is, the preaching of Christ is an act of worship to Almighty God, whether or not that preaching is received and appreciated by men.

God is well-pleased when his Son is proclaimed, whatever the reaction of the human audience may be. For God has determined that 'all should honour the Son just as they honour the Father. He who does not honour the Son does not honour the Father who sent him' (John 5:23). We honour Christ in various ways, of course — by the way we live and the way we speak, as well as by our service and worship. But it is difficult to see how we can honour Christ unless we continually and consistently proclaim him and preach his unsearchable riches (Ephesians 3:8).

Yes, God is pleased when we preach Christ — but those who are God's children also partake of his delight. Christ proclaimed is a sweet savour in their nostrils and refreshment to their souls, and they will never be truly satisfied without it. For Jesus is their 'King … a hiding place from the wind, and a covert from the tempest; as rivers of water in a dry place, as the shadow of a great rock in a weary land' (Isaiah 32:1-2). So, let Christ be preached!

2. WHAT DOES IT MEAN TO PREACH CHRIST?

'We preach Christ crucified,
to the Jews a stumbling-block
and to the Greeks foolishness,
but to those who are called, both Jews and Greeks,
Christ the power of God and the wisdom of God'
(1 Corinthians 1:23-24).

In the opening chapter I asked the question, 'What shall we preach?' The New Testament's answer is that we should 'preach Christ'. We considered some objections to this assertion, but finished by pointing out the consequence of proclaiming the Saviour — namely, to diffuse 'the fragrance of his knowledge' among men and offer a 'sweet savour of Christ' to God (2 Corinthians 2:14-15).

But what exactly does it mean to 'preach Christ'? The New Testament writers used the term freely, as if it needed no definition. But in our own days of theological confusion we would be wise to clarify its meaning. That is the purpose of this chapter and the next.

Telling good news

I pointed out that three main Greek words are translated 'preach' in our English New Testament. The first of these means to 'tell good news (or evangelise)'. The second means to 'herald' or proclaim; and the third means to 'tell thoroughly'.

In this article we consider the first of these words. It shows us that to preach Christ is to tell people the good news concerning him.

What is this good news? Let the angel reply: 'Do not be

afraid, for behold I bring you tidings of great joy … for there is born to you … a Saviour, who is Christ the Lord' (Luke 2:10-11). We preach Christ, therefore, when we present him as the One who 'will save his people from their sins' (Matthew 1:21). Let us be clear — the Christmas story is for every day and all the year!

But wait. Who says we need to be 'saved'? And what are the 'sins' we must we be saved from? Evidently, to preach Christ we must also provide answers to these questions. Sin must be defined, its origin explained. We must make clear what are the effects and consequences of sin, both in time and in eternity. If we minimise sin we devalue salvation, for it is from sin that Christ saves. He did not come to save his people from aimlessness, poverty or political adversity. He did not even come to civilise men — he came to save them.

Deliverance

In short, the good news of Jesus Christ is a message of deliverance. He 'gave himself for our sins that he might deliver us from this present evil age, according to the will of our God and Father, to whom be glory for ever and ever. Amen' (Galatians 1:4). Jesus himself announced that his mission was 'To preach deliverance to the captives …' (Luke 4:18). In preaching Christ, therefore, we must make it clear that all people are in captivity to sin and need to be delivered from its awful bondage.

Romans 6:17 puts it like this: 'God be thanked that though you were slaves of sin, yet you obeyed from the heart that form of doctrine [i.e., the gospel] to which you were delivered. And having been set free from sin, you became slaves of righteousness'. This underlines the radical nature of conversion to Christ — God has 'delivered us from the power of darkness and translated us into the kingdom of the Son of his love' (Colossians 1:13).

Needless to say, such a conversion will result in a profound transformation. In preaching Christ we should expect to see lives changed, as souls are delivered from the power of darkness and made servants of righteousness. We shall also call on those who already profess Christ to live righteously and serve as loyal subjects of Christ their King.

Diagnose and treat

However, we must never preach sin as a stand-alone subject — diagnosing corruption, applying the law, warning of judgement, and leaving people in suspense. That is not preaching Christ. Rather, we must follow the apostle in Romans 3:23-24. He first states: 'For all have sinned and fall short of the glory of God'. But he does not leave it there. Without a pause he adds: 'being justified freely by his grace through the redemption that is in Christ Jesus'.

If I am sick and visit my doctor I do not expect him to diagnose my illness and send me home. Not even if he says, 'come back next week and I will prescribe a cure'. I could be dead by then! No — diagnosis and remedy must both be supplied in a single session (though the balance between the two may well vary from one sermon to another). Without an accurate diagnosis the disease will run its course and destroy its victim. But diagnosis without treatment can be just as fatal. This applies equally whether we preach to non-believers or those who profess to believe. In Romans 1-3, admittedly, Paul is addressing the unsaved, whether Gentile or Jew. But the writer to the Hebrews uses just the same methodology in exhorting Christians. Let us see how he does it.

Warning and comfort

In Hebrews 6:1-8 we find one of the most serious warnings in the New Testament against apostasy or falling away. This is addressed to professing believers, not those outside the church. But the writer does not leave the Damocletian sword hanging over their heads. He stirs them by his warning but immediately pours in comfort — 'but, beloved', he says, 'we are confident of better things concerning you, yes, things that accompany salvation, though we speak in this manner' (Hebrews 6:9).

Whether preaching to the saved or the unsaved, the deep offensiveness of sin to God must be emphasised. But the bad news about sin and its consequences must always be accompanied by the good news concerning Christ — 'who gave himself for us, that he might redeem us from every lawless deed and purify for himself his own special people, zealous for good works' (Titus 2:14).

Repentance

In preaching the good news concerning Christ we must also preach repentance. This is much neglected in our day, when many 'believe' in Christ without any experience or understanding of repentance. Jesus commanded that 'repentance and remission of sins should be preached in his name to all nations' (Luke 24:47). He himself preached 'The kingdom of God is at hand. Repent and believe the gospel'.

On the day of Pentecost, Peter's call was for men to 'repent and ... be baptised in the name of Jesus Christ for the remission of sins' (Acts 2:38), while Paul told the Athenians that God 'commands all men everywhere to repent' and went on to proclaim the resurrection of Christ (Acts 17:18, 31).

Repentance is 'a change of mind' and a 'change of purpose' (two different Greek words are used). It is not just being sorry for sin but turning from sin as a way of life. If I am caught speeding by a police camera, I might well be sorry. But what is the long-term effect? I could get a map or satellite system showing all the speed cameras in Britain, and take care not to be caught again. Alternatively, I could change my driving habits so as to observe the speed limit whether there are cameras present or not. Only the latter pictures the life-change that is repentance.

The throne gift of Christ

But as with sin, repentance must not be preached apart from Christ. Why not? Because repentance is his throne-gift! Peter declares, 'Him God has exalted to his right hand, to be a Prince and Saviour, to give repentance to Israel and forgiveness of sins' (Acts 5:31). To preach repentance, then, we must declare that Christ is risen and exalted to God's right hand. Again, when Peter defended his visit to the Gentile Cornelius, his critics 'became silent; and they glorified God, saying, "then God has also granted to the Gentiles repentance to life"' (Acts 11:18). Even as we call on men to repent, therefore, it is essential that we point them to Christ alone as the source of repentance. Repentance and faith are alike the gifts of God.

It is because Jesus Christ is the source of all we need for salvation — repentance and faith — and because he dispenses these things from his 'glorious high throne', that Paul can 'preach Christ crucified' as 'the power of God and the wisdom of God' (1 Corinthians 1:23-24).

Christ is the power of God because he bestows salvation in sovereign grace. He is the wisdom of God because God has wisely chosen that there should be 'no other name under heaven given among men by which we must be saved' (Acts 4:12). This is good news, for we could never save ourselves from sin and the judgement it deserves.

3. TELLING THE GOOD NEWS THOROUGHLY

*'God willed to make known what are the riches of the
glory of this mystery among the Gentiles —
which is Christ in you, the hope of glory.
Him we preach,
warning every man and teaching
every man in all wisdom,
that we may present every man perfect in Christ Jesus'
(Colossians 1:28).*

In the previous chapter we began to explore the question, 'What does it mean to preach Christ?' We recalled that three main Greek verbs are rendered 'preach' in English, meaning respectively 'to tell good news', 'to tell thoroughly' and 'to herald or proclaim'. We saw first that to preach Christ is to tell the good news concerning Christ, namely, that he came to deliver his people from their sins. This required us to explain both the nature and consequences of sin and the need for repentance and faith. Moving on, we now consider the implications of the second word for preach — to tell thoroughly.

Many people advocate 'the simple gospel' which requires us to go no further than the matters considered in the previous chapter. Didn't Paul just preach 'repentance toward God, and faith toward our Lord Jesus Christ' (Acts 20:21)? No — for the passage quoted goes on to say that Paul declared 'the whole counsel of God' (Acts 20:27).

There must indeed be simplicity in our proclamation of Christ, for the gospel must be comprehensible to weak and foolish sinners like ourselves. But what passes for simplicity is often superficiality — in which the gospel is stripped of its biblical content and becomes focussed on human needs rather than divine glory. This we must avoid.

The glory of the gospel

In Colossians 1:28 (cited at the start of this chapter) Paul tells us that God's will and purpose is to 'make known the riches of the glory of the mystery'. By 'mystery' he means the gospel — once hidden but now revealed (compare Ephesians 3:4-7). This should alert us to the fact that God himself is not satisfied with a superficial message. He wants people to hear not the bare bones of the gospel but its riches and its glory!

Accordingly, Paul goes on to say, 'him [Christ] we preach' — using the Greek word *katangello* which means to 'tell thoroughly'. In other words, to preach Christ and please God we must tell people all we know about his work of redemption.

Nor should we treat this 'thorough gospel' as 'icing on the cake' — a luxury for those who enjoy rich spiritual fare but not really essential for salvation. Paul preaches Christ thoroughly to ensure that his hearers are made 'perfect [that is, complete] in Christ Jesus'. There can surely be no 'half way house' in the matter of our redemption.

A solemn responsibility

If this is the case, a most solemn responsibility rests on those who preach the Word. Paul tells Timothy, 'Meditate on these things ... take heed to yourself and to the doctrine. Continue in them, for in doing so you will save both yourself and those who hear you' (1 Timothy 4:16). This reminds us that preaching Christ involves doctrine. Not in the sense of lecturing about doctrine but in the sense that our preaching should be doctrinal in character — based on a clear view of God's eternal purpose, the Person of Christ and the meaning of the atonement.

We dare not preach Christ in a perfunctory manner. We must do justice to the 'riches' and the 'glory' — both of his Person and redeeming work. That will take time and effort, but anything less dishonours Christ and displeases God. When Paul talks about 'presenting everyone complete' he is talking about that day when 'we must all appear before the judgement seat of Christ' to give account of our lives and service (2 Corinthians 5:11-12). Trenchantly, he adds, 'Knowing therefore the terror of the Lord, we persuade men'.

Our preaching should never make anyone feel angry or uncomfortable

Or should it?

Are we serious?

But the fear of God is out of fashion. One of the great problems of our day is a lack of seriousness in preaching. There is a vogue for lightness and ease of assimilation. The best preaching, we are told, is easy on the ear and soothing for the mind. It should not make great demands upon the hearer.

Therefore it must be short, neat, and not too intense. Solid truth must be interspersed with jokes or anecdotes — sound bites are more important than sound doctrine. Our preaching must never make anyone feel angry or uncomfortable. After all, people come to church to experience the feel-good factor, don't they? This kind of thinking is endemic in many churches. Yet if we are to preach Christ thoroughly, the tendency must be resisted.

Let us return to Acts 20:26-27. Taking leave of the elders at Ephesus, Paul declared himself 'innocent of the blood of all men'. What was the basis of his confidence? The fact that he had 'not shunned to declare ... the whole counsel of God'. This is surely what it means to preach Christ thoroughly. We have no warrant to limit our preaching of Christ to those things we feel will be acceptable to men. The latter approach breeds a man-centred message — 'what Jesus can do for you if you will only let him'. Such preaching is a travesty of the gospel.

As an example of doctrinal preaching, consider the opening statement of Hebrews — that, in these last days, God has spoken to us through his Son (Hebrews 1:2). Christ is God's ultimate messenger — 'the Messenger of the Covenant' (Malachi 3:1). But what covenant is that? It is the covenant of grace and mercy established in eternity between the Father and the Son — through which God 'has saved us and called us with a holy calling, not according to our works, but according to his own purpose and grace which was given to us in Christ Jesus before time began' (2 Timothy 1:9).

Election

We cannot preach Christ thoroughly without declaring this truth — that God chose his people in Christ 'before the foundation of the world, that we should be holy and without blame before him in love' (Ephesians 1:4). Why not? Because this alone explains the nature of God's saving plan and the reason behind it. Without this information our most basic questions remain unanswered.

Yet such teaching is anathema to many Evangelicals today, and is approached with caution even by many who subscribe to 'the doctrines of grace'. Just because election is taught in Scripture, they murmur, it doesn't mean we have to preach it openly.

Should we not keep it as a 'family secret' for those who are mature enough to receive it? To tell the unsaved that God has appointed some to eternal life and not others (Acts 13:48) is surely a recipe for disaster in evangelism?

Well, if by evangelism you mean persuading sinners to 'accept' Christ by an act of their unregenerate wills, you are probably right. But if you mean proclaiming Christ to those who are dead in trespasses and sins, so that they might be quickened to life by the power of the Holy Spirit, you are wrong. The doctrine of election humbles proud sinners (who otherwise think they can save themselves) and glorifies Christ (who alone can do so). It is fundamental to our whole understanding of salvation by grace.

The glory of God's grace

I do not mean, of course, that this doctrine must always feature prominently in evangelism, as if it were the central thing. The heart of Paul's message to the Athenians, for example, was 'Jesus and the resurrection', and to the Corinthians, 'Jesus Christ and him crucified' (Acts 17:18; 1 Corinthians 2:2). Nor am I saying it is mandatory to mention election in every sermon or evangelistic message. But unless our preaching sets God's saving work in the context of his eternal counsels, we are not preaching Christ thoroughly — for he is the Messenger of the everlasting covenant, without which there would be no grace and no salvation.

Nor, if we neglect this eternal dimension of salvation, are we giving God the glory that is due to his name. For when Paul lists 'every spiritual blessing' bestowed upon us by the gospel, he includes election, predestination, adoption, acceptance in the Beloved, and redemption through Christ's blood — all designed to celebrate and honour 'the praise of the glory of his grace' (Ephesians 1:3-7). It is only 'the grace of God that brings salvation', and this grace 'has appeared to all men' (Titus 2:11). It is not something God wishes to conceal, as if he were somehow ashamed of its implications. No more shall we conceal it if we preach Christ thoroughly.

4. THE UNSEARCHABLE RICHES OF CHRIST

'To me, who am less than the least of all the saints,
this grace was given,
that I should preach among the Gentiles
the unsearchable riches of Christ, and to make all people
see what is the fellowship of the mystery which from the
beginning of the ages has been hidden in God
who created all things through Jesus Christ'
(Ephesians 3:8-9).

The previous chapter proposed that to 'preach Christ' faithfully we must preach him thoroughly. That is the significance of the Greek word *katangello*, one of the three major terms translated 'preach' in our English New Testament. To preach nothing 'except Christ and him crucified' (1 Corinthians 2:2) might at first seem restrictive, but our text (above) proves otherwise. Were we to preach Christ for a million years we would never exhaust the subject. Why not? Because his riches are unsearchable — too vast to be fully explored.

Some are afraid that such preaching will demand too much from our hearers. Unless we keep it simple, they warn, we shall frighten off those who are theologically untrained.

But such fears are groundless. To whom did Paul preach Christ's unsearchable riches? To the theologically illiterate Gentiles! Did he share the fellowship of the mystery (the 'gospel secret') only with some spiritual elite? No, he shared it with 'all people'!

The message of Christ's inexhaustible riches should be proclaimed to everyone, even though all will not receive it (see 2 Corinthians 2:14-16).

Every spiritual blessing

What, then, are these unsearchable treasures, and where are they found, that we might preach them? In reply, I want to cite two New Testament passages where Christ's riches are set before us.

I do not mean that these riches reside only in selected Scriptures. That is not so. Wherever Christ is found in Scripture, there also lie his riches. But certain passages are particularly helpful because they read almost like inventories of his wealth. They therefore show us what to look for as we seek this wealth 'in all the Scriptures'.

Let us begin where we finished the last chapter, in Ephesians 1:1-14. Paul whets our appetite in verse 3 when he writes, 'Blessed be the God and Father of our Lord Jesus Christ, who has blessed us with every spiritual blessing in the heavenly places in Christ'. These spiritual blessings form a substantial part of Christ's riches. What are they?

The first is election — '[The Father] chose us in [Christ] before the foundation of the world' (v.4). How does this enrich us? Romans 8:28-29 explains. God's choice or foreknowledge of his people is the foundation of all we possess and hope for in Christ. It undergirds our assurance of salvation (we have a pre-ordained destination), our calling, our justification and our eventual glorification. Moreover, it is the basis of our present comfort and confidence, knowing that 'all things work together for good to those who love God ... who are *called according to his purpose*'.

Predestined in love

But Ephesians 1:4-5 does not stop there. Paul explains the purpose for which we were chosen — 'that we should be holy and without blame before him in love, [God] having predestined us to adoption as sons by Jesus Christ to himself'. God chose us that he might adopt us as his children. That is the destination he has purposed for redeemed sinners. Notice that Scripture never uses the verb 'predestine' without specifying the intended 'destination' — in this case, the new-covenant status of sons and daughters of God (Hebrews 2:10; 8:9-12). Looked at in this light, predestination ceases to be a 'bogy' word and becomes the glorious guarantee that God will fulfil his loving purpose towards us.

Furthermore, to fit us for this purpose — as a means to this end — he has made us 'holy and without blame' through the atoning work of Christ. And all this he carries out 'in love', for love is the wellspring of everything God does for his people.

What riches we have here! Loved with everlasting love; chosen in undeserved grace; robed in the righteousness of Christ; adopted and endowed as God's children; and destined for eternal glory! Here are themes to fill our mouths and engage our hearts.

Riches of grace

The following verses (Ephesians 1:6-14) spread before us 'the riches of his grace' — according to which we are 'accepted in the beloved', redeemed through Christ's blood, and forgiven our sins. This grace is not only *extended* to us, but *lavished* upon us — God made it 'abound towards us in all wisdom and prudence'. Furthermore, through this same grace, God reveals to us his ultimate purpose, namely, 'to gather together in one all things in Christ (v.10).

Have you finished, Paul? Not at all! For the culmination of this cascade of glory is now revealed — God's children 'have obtained an inheritance, being predestined [to this inheritance] according to the purpose of him who works all things according to the counsel of his will' (v.11). And to cap it all, we have been 'sealed with the Holy Spirit of promise, who is the guarantee of our inheritance ...' (v.14).

It seems to me that these verses in Ephesians define the riches of Christ in a manner that invites the preacher to delve deeper into them and his hearers to bask in their warmth and light. Some thirteen blessings are here recorded, each of which offer limitless scope for worship, exploration and delight — 'to the praise of the glory of [God's] grace'.

All the fullness

A second passage that delineates the riches of Christ is Colossians 1:9-23. Once again we can only sketch the good things here displayed. The passage begins in a practical mode, as Paul prays for his readers to be 'filled with the knowledge of [God's] will in all wisdom and spiritual understanding' (v.1). Believers share their Master's wealth in knowing the Father's will — in all its fullness, wisdom and spiritual awareness. 'Receive my instruction and not silver', declares Solomon, 'And knowledge rather than choice gold. For wisdom is better than rubies, and all the things one may desire cannot be compared with her' (Proverbs 8:10-11).

In Christ, we are told, 'are hidden all the treasures of wisdom and knowledge' (Colossians 2:3). We do well to search out these riches in our preaching, for quite apart from their intrinsic worth they will enable us to 'live a life worthy of the Lord, fully pleasing him, being fruitful in every good work and increasing in the knowledge of God' (v.10). Read on to see how these riches of knowledge give rise to strength (according to God's glorious power), patience, joy and thanksgiving (vv. 11-12).

Head of the church

Yet Paul has only just begun! In verse 12 we discover that 'the Father ... has qualified us to be partakers of the inheritance of the saints in the light'. Verse 13 tells us that we have been 'delivered ... from the power of darkness and translated into the kingdom' of Christ, where 'we have redemption through his blood'. What wealth is here!

But then, in a sense-shattering passage, from verses 14-20, the full glories of Christ's person and work burst upon us. He is 'the image of the invisible God', the 'first-born over all creation'. He is the one through whom and for whom all things were created, and in whom all things consist. At the same time, Paul continues, he is 'the head of the body, the church' and 'the firstborn from the dead, that in all things he might have the pre-eminence — for it pleased the Father than in him all the fullness should dwell' (vv. 18-19). The 'fullness' referred to is nothing less that that of the Godhead itself (2:9). You cannot get richer than that!

Accessing the riches

A third passage we could have turned to is Hebrews 1:1-4, but space forbids. The point I want to reiterate is that passages such as these should not be regarded as the treasure casket itself (though they are part of it) but rather as the key to the casket. We can take any of the numerous themes broached in these passages and explore them throughout the Scriptures using nothing more complicated than our memory, our concordance or our Bible software.

For example, the very words 'riches' or 'treasures' will yield dozens of references, including such Scriptures as Proverbs 8:18 — 'Riches and honour are with me; yea, durable riches and righteousness', and Isaiah 45:3 — 'I will give you the treasures of darkness and hidden riches of secret places, that you may know that I, the LORD, who call you by your name, am the God of Israel'.

Both texts provide a fruitful starting point for preaching Christ, in whom alone true riches and honour are found, and in whom the treasures of the gospel await our discovery.

5. PREACHING THE ATONEMENT

*'And I, brethren, when I came to you, did not come with
excellence of speech or of wisdom declaring to you the
testimony of God. For I determined not to know anything
among you except Jesus Christ and him crucified'*
(1 Corinthians 2:1-2).

We have just explored what it means to 'preach the unsearchable
riches of Christ' (Ephesians 3:8) but we cannot leave this subject
without dealing specifically with our Lord's atoning work. When
the apostles preached Christ they proclaimed his death, his
resurrection and his exaltation — and these things are foremost
among the riches made available to us in Christ. In this chapter
we have space to consider only the death of Christ.

Christ crucified

When Paul brought the gospel to Corinth he 'determined' to
preach nothing but 'Christ and him crucified' (text above). 'We
preach Christ crucified', he declared, 'to the Jews a stumbling-
block and to the Greeks foolishness, but to those who are called,
both Jews and Greeks, Christ the power of God and the wisdom
of God' (1 Corinthians 1:23-24). Do not imagine that Paul nar-
rowed his message when he went to Corinth. On the contrary,
the atoning work of Christ has such vast implications that it
embraces the infinite treasures of grace.

Paul could have won favour among the Greeks by adorning
(and diluting!) his message with human philosophy. He could
have gained respect among the Jews by mingling his new covenant gospel with Judaism. But he refused to pander to man's

religious or intellectual pride. He had no desire to diminish 'the offence of the cross' (Galatians 5:11). Why? Because only the message of the cross could save them and bring them to experience 'the power of God and the wisdom of God'. This is highly relevant to our own situation. Many think the gospel can only succeed if it accommodates the wishes of the world. Do people want intellectual stimulation? Then give them philosophy. Do they desire ritual? Then model your worship on the Mosaic tabernacle and priesthood. Do they seek emotional release and inner healing? Then give them psychological stimuli — music, dancing, participation — whatever works for them. But Paul knew better. He preached a message that offended the world — yet drew those who were 'called' by the gospel and the Spirit of God.

Who killed Christ?

What, then, should we preach concerning the death of Christ? At very least, the following five things: Firstly, that God himself was responsible for the crucifixion. On the day of Pentecost, Peter declared, 'Him being delivered by the carefully planned intention and foreknowledge of God, you have taken by lawless hands, have crucified and put to death' (Acts 2:23). Of course, the Jews and Romans of that day were guilty. But their guilt was representative — a guilt that attaches to humanity in general, not to any race or nation in particular. More importantly, however, the cross was 'the carefully planned intention' of God himself. Jesus Christ was 'the Lamb slain from the foundation of the world' (Revelation 13:8). His death as a sacrifice for sin was determined long before there *were* any Jews or Romans — in the eternal counsels of God. Christ's crucifixion was not 'death by misadventure' nor could it stem ultimately from human actions, no matter how wicked and perverse. Zechariah makes it clear: "'Awake, O sword, against my Shepherd, against the Man who is my companion", says the Lord of hosts: "Strike the Shepherd and the sheep will be scattered"' (Zechariah 13:7; compare Mark 14:27). God's righteous judgement fell on Christ.

Why did Christ have to die?

Secondly, our preaching must explain why Jesus was condemned to die in this way. We have already touched upon the answer. Christ was 'the lamb of God who takes away the sin of the world' (John 1:29). Put simply, Christ was an innocent substitute, sacrificed to make atonement (satisfaction) for sin. From Abel onwards, animal sacrifices were offered to placate God's righteous anger and atone for human sin. The symbolism reached its zenith under the Mosaic covenant when, day by day and year by year, an unending parade of animals died to keep God's wrath at bay. Unchanging principles were involved — an animal without blemish died in the place of the human sinner to propitiate God's wrath against sin and free the transgressor from guilt and punishment. That is what we mean by 'atonement'. The Old Testament itself speaks prophetically of Christ: 'Surely he has borne our griefs and carried our sorrows. Yet we esteemed him stricken, smitten by God, and afflicted. But he was wounded for our transgressions, he was bruised for our iniquities; the chastisement for our peace was upon him, and by his stripes we are healed' (Isaiah 53:4-5).

The idea of atonement is fundamental to our approach to God. Without it we can neither enter his presence nor enjoy any relationship with him — for we are sinful and he is holy beyond comprehension. 'But now in Christ Jesus [we] who once were far off have been brought near by the blood of Christ' (Ephesians 2:13). If knowing God is man's supreme joy, then the atoning work of Christ that makes such knowledge possible must surely be surpassing wealth. Paul puts it thus: 'For you know the grace of our Lord Jesus Christ, that though he was rich, yet for your sakes he became poor, that you through his poverty might become rich' (2 Corinthians 8:9; see also 5:21).

Victory over sin and Satan

Thirdly, believers are not only reconciled to God by the death of his Son, but are also given victory over sin. Peter writes of Christ that he 'bore our sins in his own body on the tree, that we, having died to sins, might live for righteousness — by whose stripes you were healed' (1 Peter 2:24). We impoverish ourselves if we put a full stop after the word 'tree'. For Christ not only died for our sins but took our sinful selves to crucifixion with him. 'Our old man was crucified with him that ... we should no longer be slaves of sin, for he who has died has been freed from sin' (Romans 6:6-7).

By what power are we freed from sin? By the power of the indwelling Spirit of Christ — 'I am crucified with Christ', declares Paul. 'It is no longer I who live, but Christ lives in me' (Galatians 2:20). Jesus' death also brings victory over Satan, for we read that God's Son became man 'that through death he might destroy him who had the power of death, that is the devil' (Hebrews 2:14; see also Colossians 2:15). Paul works out the practical application of these liberating truths in Romans 6:11-22, culminating with the words: 'having been set free from sin, and having become slaves of God, you have your fruit to holiness, and the end, everlasting life'.

Our great high priest

Fourthly, we must proclaim Christ as our great high priest. He was not only the sacrificial lamb, but also the one who willingly offered himself to redeem us — 'Neither by the blood of goats and calves, but by his own blood he entered in once into the holy place, having obtained eternal redemption for us' (Hebrews 9:12).

Christ's high priestly office opens up a vein of pure gold for the believer — a vein the preacher ought to mine with overflowing joy. In his sublime role of high priest, Christ is our representative (Hebrews 2:9), our forerunner (Hebrews 6:20), our peace-maker (Colossians 1:20), our intercessor (Hebrews 7:25), our acceptance (Ephesians 1:6), our sanctification (Hebrews 10:10), and the one who perfects us for ever (Hebrews 10:14). Furthermore, when Jesus entered the ineffable presence of Almighty God, bearing his own blood, he opened the way for us to follow — 'Therefore, brethren, having boldness to enter the Holy Place by the blood of Jesus ... by a new and living way ... and having a high priest over the house of God ... let us draw near ...' (Hebrews 10:19-22). No wealth could be greater.

The eternal inheritance

Fifthly, we must declare that Christ's death bestows on his elect an eternal inheritance. Hebrews describes this incalculable benefit: 'He is the mediator of the new covenant, by means of death, for the redemption of the transgressions under the first covenant, that those who are called may receive the promise of the eternal inheritance. For where there is a testament, there must also of necessity be the death of the testator' (Hebrews 9:15-17). The inheritance in question is 'the kingdom prepared for [God's people] from the foundation of the world' (Matthew 25:34). But although it was prepared before time began, it could not be possessed unless (and until) Christ was glorified in death.

The cross of Christ is therefore our passport to this kingdom. Its citizenship cannot be purchased with 'corruptible things like silver and gold' but only with 'the precious blood of Christ, as of a lamb without blemish and without spot' (1 Peter 1:18-19). It was he who, 'with his own blood, entered the Most Holy Place once for all, having obtained eternal redemption' (Hebrews 9:12). Such are the riches of Christ's atoning, sanctifying, redeeming death. Dare we not preach them? And what of the riches of his resurrection, his ascension, his enthronement, his power, his glory, his triumph ...? Sadly, time and space forbid. But one thing is certain. Those who preach Christ thoroughly will never lack a message to thrill the hearts of needy sinners.

6. HERALDING THE SAVIOUR

*' Casting down arguments and
every high thing that exalts itself against
the knowledge of God,
bringing every thought into captivity to
the obedience of Christ'
(2 Corinthians 10:5).*

In earlier chapters we have considered two of the Greek words translated 'to preach' in our English Bibles — one meaning to 'tell good news (evangelise)' and another 'to tell thoroughly'. We saw how these words relate to the preaching of Christ. The third common Greek verb translated 'preach' means to herald or proclaim, and it has an interesting history. In and before New Testament times a herald had various functions. One of these was to call together an assembly for the purpose of making a pronouncement. Another was to act as an intermediary between opposing forces — for example, to convey terms of surrender to an embattled army and bring back their reply. 'Heralds were believed to be the messengers of the gods. They carried wands; their persons were inviolable, and they were regarded as the messengers, and under the protection, of Jove' (Liddell and Scott Greek lexicon).

Christian usage

When the early church needed a word to describe the preaching of the gospel they chose (among others) a verb derived from 'herald'. No doubt their main intention was to convey the idea of `proclamation´ but the other heraldic functions are also relevant, as we shall see.

Firstly, then, to preach Christ we must proclaim Christ. Even today Heralds are sometimes used on ceremonial occasions to announce a monarch or other dignitary. A trumpet fanfare greets their arrival, silencing idle chatter and drawing all eyes to the one proclaimed. So it is with Christ. The purpose of preaching is to herald his appearance, `bringing all thoughts into captivity to the obedience of Christ` (2 Corinthians 10:5). This, at least, should be the effect that preaching Christ has upon our hearers, namely, to focus their attention on his glorious Person and saving work.

It is not the herald's task to invite people to a discussion, forum or debate. Nor is it to entertain the audience with music or display his instrumental virtuosity. The herald's function is to announce that a person of great authority or rank stands before the gathered throng. So also, when we herald Christ there is but one purpose — to make everyone look to him and wait upon his words. The preacher must have a genuine desire that 'he must increase and [we] must decrease' (John 3:30). Paul could say, 'We preach not ourselves but Christ Jesus the Lord, and ourselves your servants for Jesus sake' (2 Corinthians 4:5). Although we pay lip service to this principle we do not always observe it in practice. The preacher is constantly tempted to promote himself in various ways — to exhibit his skill and erudition or 'play to the gallery'. And the temptation increases the more successful we become. It takes great grace and humility to truly preach Christ rather than ourselves. But the difference will show.

Uncertain sounds

But what if 'the trumpet makes an uncertain sound' (1 Corinthians 14:8)? Sadly, this often happens. Some preaching lacks clarity because the preacher is afraid to 'declare the whole counsel of

God' (Acts 20:27). Paul implies that this was a problem even in his own day, asking the Galatians, 'Do I now appease men or God?' (Galatians 1:10. See also his dispute with Peter in Galatians 2:11-14). Too often, 'the fear of man brings a snare' (Proverbs 29:25). We are afraid to speak clearly in case we offend people by doctrines that debase human pride and exalt the sovereign power of God.

Some years ago I was asked to read a manuscript submitted for publication on the pastoral ministry. The would-be author suggested that a pastor appointed to a new church should not mention the doctrines of grace for about two years and should then introduce them very gradually. Otherwise, he said, people would reject the teaching and leave the church (the manuscript was rejected!). But our task as heralds is not to please men but to promote the knowledge of Christ. Of course, this must be done gently and graciously, 'with all patience and doctrine' (2 Timothy 4:2). But it must also be done with great clarity and biblical authority.

Relating all to Christ

But perhaps more often the preaching 'makes an uncertain sound' because the preacher himself is confused about the need to proclaim Christ or how to do so. These chapters are intended, of course, to help resolve any lack of clarity in these things. In practical terms, when preparing a sermon, Bible study or Sunday School lesson, we should always ask ourselves what the message will teach its hearers about Christ and their need of him — his Person, his redeeming work, his grace, his love, his compassion, his example and so much else.

How early in the message do we intend to introduce Christ? How soon will we mention his name? How quickly will he engage the attention of our hearers? If our topic is historical in nature, how will we tie this into the history of redemption? If our subject is 'worship', how central to our concept of 'divine service' will Christ be made? If we are concerned with ecclesiology, how does our subject-matter relate to the church as Christ's 'body, the fullness of him who fills all in all' (Ephesians 1:23)? If our message deals with practical living and morality, or with family life, do we see Christ as the source of our wisdom — and his indwelling Spirit as our enabling power — in all such matters? And so we could continue. If we want to guide our hearers aright, the compass needle of our thoughts must constantly return to Christ.

Spirit-given authority

But what of the other aspects of the heraldic function? Firstly, in pagan society heralds were regarded as messengers of the gods, endowed with the protection and authority of those deities. Did the New Testament writers have this in mind also when they chose to speak of 'heralding the gospel'? We do not know. But they certainly believed that those who preach Christ do so with the full authority of God. Peter writes of 'those who have preached the gospel to you by the Holy Spirit sent from heaven' (1 Peter 1:12). What do we know of this divine, Spirit-given authority in our preaching today? More to the point, how may we know it? The answer, surely, is that in our preaching we must let the Spirit of God speak through his own Word.

Too often our preaching is a statement of our own beliefs and opinions. These may be doctrinally impeccable, but if we fail to let the message emerge from the Scriptures themselves, we shall speak in our own authority, not God's. Furthermore, it must be clear to our hearers that our teaching arises naturally from God's word — otherwise they may discern the wisdom of man rather than the voice of God. It is vital, therefore, that before we preach we should meditate deeply on the Scripture passage(s) involved. We must ourselves listen before we dare to speak, asking such things as these. What would the Lord say to us through this Scripture? Where in the passage is Christ delineated? How will the Spirit of God fulfil his work of glorifying Christ by taking of the things of Christ and declaring them — first to the preacher and then to the people (John 16:14)? Unless the Spirit speaks, the authority of our preaching will be human, not divine.

Terms of surrender

Finally, the herald of old carried messages between warring armies — not least the terms of surrender offered to an embattled foe. So also the gospel preacher conveys God's terms of surrender to rebel sinners. 'Repent of your sins and believe on the Lord Jesus Christ, and you will be saved!' Let us understand that God sets the terms. The gospel of Christ is an invitation (Matthew 11:29-30) but it is also a command (Acts 17:20-21). It is never a compromise with worldliness or sin, or with the inclinations of the rebel heart and mind. It calls for total surrender for obedience to the gospel and submission to the righteousness of God (1 Peter 1:2; Romans 10:3).

In our preaching we must reason with sinners (Acts 24:25) and answer their questions (1 Peter 3:15), but we must not debate with them as if the truth of the gospel were negotiable. Nor can we be apologetic or evasive concerning what God requires in terms of faith and submission to the gospel. Men must come to Christ on his terms, not their own, and it is the preacher's responsibility to make those terms crystal clear. As they do so come, they will find that God is gracious beyond their wildest dreams. And, as we have seen, they will begin to discover the unsearchable riches of Christ.

7. DID JESUS PREACH CHRIST?

*'And he opened their understanding
that they might comprehend
the Scriptures.
Then he said to them,
"Thus it is written and thus it was
necessary for the Christ to suffer
and to rise from the dead
the third day, and that repentance
and remission of sins should be
preached in his name
to all nations …"'
(Luke 24:45-47).*

Our study of 'preaching Christ' has concentrated on what we might call 'apostolic preaching', that is, preaching after Pentecost. This must be our primary pattern because we live today in the era following the coming of the Holy Spirit. The disciples were actually forbidden to begin their preaching ministry until the 'promise of the Father' — the gift of the Spirit — had come upon them (Acts 1:4-5). Only then could they be effective witnesses to Christ and his gospel. But this does not mean that pre-Pentecostal preaching has no bearing on our subject, for both John the Baptist and Jesus himself preached Christ! Consider first and briefly the testimony of John.

John the Baptist

If asked, 'What did John preach?' many Christians would reply, 'He preached repentance'. We are told that John 'went into all the region around the Jordan preaching a baptism of repentance for the remission of sins' (Luke 3:3). In harmony with this message he gave clear and practical instructions concerning repentant life-styles to those who sought his baptism (Luke 3:10-14). Furthermore, John's baptism was not Christian baptism. We know this from Paul's experience at Ephesus — where he encountered some disciples who knew only the baptism of John and re-baptised them 'in the name of the Lord Jesus' (Acts 19:1-7).

Nevertheless, as we read the New Testament account it becomes plain that John came to prepare the way for Christ, in fulfilment of Isaiah's prophecy (Luke 3:4-6). He was sent 'to bear witness of that light' — which light was Christ (John 1: 8,15). He preached repentance for the same reason Jesus preached repentance, that is, because the kingdom of God was at hand (Mark 1:15). It was 'at hand', of course, in the person of Jesus of Nazareth. Accordingly, John proclaimed Christ as the coming Lord, the Son of God — one preferred before himself who would baptise, not with water, but with the Holy Spirit and with fire. One who would increase as John himself decreased. Above all, he memorably identified Jesus as 'the lamb of God who takes away the sin of the world' (John 1:29-36). There can be no question that John the Baptist preached Christ.

What did Jesus preach?

But what of Jesus himself? His utterances constitute the largest body of teaching and preaching by a single person in the New Testament and we clearly cannot ignore it! Although it was a pre-Pentecostal ministry, the Holy Spirit came upon Jesus at his baptism. Unlike the disciples, he had no need to wait for that anointing. What, then, did Jesus preach? It may sound odd to say that he preached himself, but that is exactly the conclusion to which we are led! To demonstrate this contention I want us to consider briefly (1) the fulfilment of prophecy; (2) the 'I am' passages in John's gospel; (3) the sermon on the mount; (4) the parables; and (5) the great commission.

Firstly, Jesus declared himself to be the promised Messiah by claiming to fulfil Old Testament prophecy. Perhaps the best known example of this is the discourse on the road to Emmaus where, 'beginning at Moses and all the prophets he expounded to them in all the Scriptures the things concerning himself' (Luke 24:27). We shall have more to say about this incident when we come to consider preaching Christ from the Old Testament later in this booklet. An equally important state-ment, however, is made at the very beginning of Jesus' public ministry, in the synagogue at Nazareth. He reads from Isaiah 61 and declares, 'today this scripture is fulfilled in your hearing' (Luke 4:17-21). He is

even more direct with the Samaritan woman in John 4. 'I know that Messiah is coming ... when he comes he will tell us all things', she declared. 'I who speak to you am he', replied the Saviour.

These unambiguous claims to be the 'anointed one' of OT prophecy amounted to a self-proclamation of enormous significance. Peter spoke for all the disciples when he testi-fied, 'You are the Christ, the Son of the living God' (Matthew 16:16). His enemies were equally moved by the claim but they responded with murderous hatred and accusations of blasphemy (Luke 4:23-30).

Secondly, Jesus preached himself as the Christ by making a series of breathtaking claims, which John records in the famous 'I am' passages. Jesus pronounced himself to be 'the bread of life' that gives life to the soul (John 6:15); 'the light of the world' that scatters the sinner's darkness (8:12); 'the door' to salvation (10:9); 'the good shepherd' who gives his life for the sheep (10:11); 'the resurrection and the life' giving eternal life and ultimate redemption to all who believe in him (11:25-26); 'the way, the truth and the life' through whom alone a person may approach and know the living God (14:6); and 'the true vine' in whom believers both live and bear 'much fruit' to God (15:5). Could there be any clearer preaching of Christ than this? Surely not, for in these sayings (and the sermons he built around them) Jesus delineates his whole ministry of reconciling sinners to God and giving them eternal life.

The Sermon on the Mount

We turn now to a very different kind of preaching — Jesus' famous Sermon on the Mount (Matthew 5-7). At first sight this sermon (the longest recorded in the New Testament) is a handbook of Christian living, though it clearly contains evangelistic elements as well. Where, then, is Christ preached in this message? The answer is found at the conclusion of the sermon, where Jesus recounts the familiar parable of the two houses, one built on the rock and the other on sand. What is the point of this story? Listen to the preacher: 'Whoever hears these sayings of mine and does them, I will liken him to a wise man who built his house on the rock … everyone who hears these sayings of mine and does not do them, will be like a foolish man who built his house on the sand' (Matthew 7:24-27).

Jesus is teaching here the fundamental nature of what he calls 'these sayings of mine', basing the whole edifice of Christian morality and life-practice upon his own supreme authority. The importance of this to the Christian life is seldom fully appreciated. A life built upon Christ's teaching in this sermon is secure because it submits to the authority of the Son of God. A life that is not so built is likely to be forfeit, whatever other rules of life it might follow. Matthew 7:21-23 makes it clear that calling Christ 'Lord' is not enough — we must also *obey* him as Lord.

For example, as Matthew 5:21-22 demonstrates, a person whose rule of life embraces no more than an outward obedience to the commandment 'You shall not murder', and who ignores Christ's warning against hating or despising others, is building on sand, not rock. The one who impeccably avoids adultery but lusts in his heart is condemned, not commended (Matthew 5:27-30). It is good to disown theft and covetousness, but unless we go further and act generously towards those in need, we are disobeying Christ and building on sand (Matthew 5:42). In the Sermon on the Mount, therefore, Jesus asserts his ultimate personal authority over all matters of morality and behaviour — and spells out the consequences of neglecting to heed his divine instruction. This is 'Christ centred preaching' at its most practical and powerful level.

The parables

The parables of Jesus form an important part of his teaching. At certain times he appears to have taught almost exclusively in parables (Matthew 13:14) while at others he used parables to drive home lessons he also stated in plain speech (as in the parables of the houses built on rock and sand, and the unjust judge). A significant number of the parables 'preach Christ' directly. The parable of the wicked vine-dressers describes the Jews' rejection and murder of the Son of God. Several parables picture his second coming and warn of judgement, such as the parables of the talents, the fig tree, the wise and foolish virgins and the sheep and the goats.

In the parable of the tares, it is the Son of Man who first sows the seed and later sends his angels to gather out of his kingdom 'all things that offend' (Matthew 13:37,41). Probably the most famous parable of all is that of the sower and the seed (Matthew 13:3-23 also in Mark and Luke). At first sight this refers to any sower of the word and makes no specific mention of Christ. But what is 'the word' if it is not the message of Christ's kingdom? The whole parable, says Jesus, relates to 'the mysteries of the kingdom of heaven' and goes on to say that these mysteries were being revealed to his own disciples in a way that they were not previously revealed to 'many prophets and righteous men' (Matthew 13:11,17). Clearly, Jesus here sets himself forward as the One who reveals these 'kingdom secrets' to his own, and we are reminded of Hebrews 1:2; 'God ... has in these last days spoken to us by his Son'.

In Luke 15, Christ is the woman who searches diligently for her lost coin; the shepherd who seeks and finds his lost sheep; and even the 'everlasting father' of Isaiah 9:6 who welcomes back his renegade son. He is the merchant of Matthew 13:45-46 who (on one interpretation) gives his all to purchase the pearl of great price, namely, his church. He is the bridegroom at the wedding (Matthew 22:1-14) — and so we could continue. Either directly or indirectly, every parable presents us with the Person, work and glory of the Lord Jesus Christ.

The great commission

Finally, as his last action here upon earth, the risen Christ gave his church its 'marching orders' — the great commission. But what is this commission? Luke tells us: 'he opened their understanding that they might comprehend the Scriptures. Then he said to them, "Thus it is written and thus it was necessary for the Christ to suffer and to rise from the dead the third day, and that repentance and remission of sins should be preached in his name to all nations … "' (Luke 24:45-47).

These verses testify again, of course, that OT Scripture looks forward to the work of Christ. But they also demonstrate that the church's task in this world is to preach repentance and forgiveness in Christ's name. What does that mean? Matthew 28:18-20 elucidates. We are to 'make disciples' of Christ from all nations, teaching them 'all things that [Christ] commanded'. The only way to do that is to preach Christ in his fullness, as Saviour, Lord and coming King. The great commission could thus be described as the great proclamation of Christ. He did not tell his disciples to preach philosophy, morality or the law — they were to preach him, his saving work and the glory of his kingdom. Wherever Christ is preached and his disciples gathered out of all nations, there will be a Christian philosophy or world-view; there will be moral righteousness; and God's law will be obeyed from the heart. But unless we prioritise the preaching of 'Christ and him crucified' none of these things can come about.

8. PREACHING CHRIST
TO CHRISTIANS

'Him we preach, warning every man
and teaching every man in all wisdom,
that we may present every man perfect in Christ Jesus'
(Colossians 1:28).

We now turn to a subject that is in some ways contentious — do we need to preach Christ to those who are already believers? Some will point out that most Bible references to preaching Christ are found in the context of missions and evangelism. Clearly, to preach the gospel to the unsaved we must preach Christ. But do believers need something different?

I touched on this question in the first chapter of this booklet, and made a preliminary point from Hebrews 12:1-2. If believers are to 'run with endurance ... looking to Jesus', then surely they must be both helped and exhorted to do so. And how can we do that apart from preaching Christ? — for he is both the author of faith and its perfector, and we are complete in him (Colossians 2:10). Let us consider this further.

Majoring on Christ

Without question, the epistle to the Hebrews was written to Christians. Although the writer warns his readers against apostasy, he clearly believes them to be truly saved (Hebrews 6:9). It is also obvious that the epistle is a homily — a sermon in writing — full of Bible exposition, application and exhortation. Yet what is the subject of Hebrews if it is not Christ? It presents him as the eternal Son and express image of God; it sets him before us as the creator, sustainer and heir of all things. It unveils the incarnate Christ as the representative man; as the high priest and mediator of the new covenant; and so much more.

If the Hebrews needed such sustained (even repetitive) teaching concerning Christ then so, surely, do we. The same can be said of the recipients of all the New Testament epistles, for even the most practical of them 'majors' on Christ. The reason for this emphasis is clear: 'Him we preach, warning every man and teaching every man in all wisdom, that we may present every man *perfect in Christ Jesus*' (Colossians 1:28). Note the emphasis I have added. Christians can only be brought to completeness (perfection) if they learn of Christ.

Isolated texts

Of course, we can iso-
late texts that contain
no reference to Christ.
I remember hearing
a sermon on 1 Cor-
inthians 5:33 — 'Evil
company corrupts good
habits' — in which the
preacher talked exclu-

Feed my sheep

sively about the moral dangers of keeping bad company! Yet this statement is part of Paul's extended treatment of the resurrection of Christ and its implications for believers. The apostle warns the Corinthians to distance themselves from those who implicitly deny the resurrection of Christ (1 Corinthians 15:12-19). In fact this passage begins with the words, 'Now if Christ is preached that he has been raised from the dead, how do some among you say that there is no resurrection of the dead?' No excuse here, then, for not preaching Christ!

This illustrates the danger of preaching from isolated texts without giving due consideration to the context. I would suggest that throughout the New Testament, whatever the immediate concern of the writer, the context is always Christological. The preacher has a responsibility to set his text firmly in this context and thus relate the subject matter of his sermon to Christ.

The pastoral epistles

Three NT epistles were written specifically to help church leaders pastor their flocks — two to Timothy and one to Titus. Although pastors also 'do the work of an evangelist' (2 Timothy 4:5) their chief duty as elders is to 'shepherd [feed] the flock of God which is among you' (1 Peter 5:1-4). The pastoral epistles are full of practical teaching concerning the life of the local church — teaching that is much needed in our own day. But Paul is careful to emphasise two things. Firstly, pastors are to teach these things by preaching to believers: 'I charge you therefore before God and the Lord Jesus Christ ... preach the word! ... Convince, rebuke, exhort, with all long-suffering and teaching' (2 Timothy 4:1-2).

Secondly, the purpose of such teaching, no matter how practical and down-to-earth it might be, is that believers should 'adorn the doctrine of God our Saviour in all things' — for 'Christ ... gave himself for us that he might redeem us from every lawless deed and purify for himself his own special people, zealous for good works' (Titus 2:10, 17-19). In other words, all practical and moral teaching has the aim of fulfilling God's purpose in Christ. As Peter puts it: 'You are a chosen generation, a royal priesthood, a holy nation, his own special people, that you may proclaim the praises of him who called you out of darkness into his marvellous light' (1 Peter 2:9). To teach ethics and morality, church life and obedience, without reference to their purpose of 'adorning the doctrine' and glorifying Christ, is to put the cart before the horse (or even to discard the horse altogether).

Foundation

But is not the Sermon on the Mount a moral treatise without reference to Christ himself? Not at all. Near the beginning of the sermon Jesus makes it clear that he came to fulfil 'the law and the prophets' (Matthew 5:17). The sermon proceeds to unveil what God requires of man — gathering up and going beyond the teaching of the Old Testament. For example, although the OT tells us to take pity on our enemies (Proverbs 25:21-22), nowhere does it say we have to love them (Matthew 5:43-48)! Again, at the end of the sermon, Christ reveals himself and his teaching as the foundational 'rock' on which our lives must be built if they are to withstand the storms of life and judgement (Matthew 7:24-29).

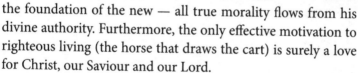

We cannot preach the moral requirements of God, therefore, without reference to Christ. He is both the fulfilment of the old covenant and the foundation of the new — all true morality flows from his divine authority. Furthermore, the only effective motivation to righteous living (the horse that draws the cart) is surely a love for Christ, our Saviour and our Lord.

Sweet savour

Above all, however, we should preach Christ to Christians because nothing else can satisfy the true believer. 'To you who believe', says Peter, 'he is precious'. Why? Because God says, 'Behold, I lay in Zion a chief cornerstone, elect, precious, and he who believes on him will by no means be put to shame' (1 Peter 2:6-7). This being so, to fail to proclaim Christ to believers is to rob them of that which brings them greatest joy. It deprives them of the 'fragrance of his knowledge' and the 'sweet savour of Christ ... of life unto life' (2 Corinthians 2:14-17; KJV).

If Christ is the bread of life, the manna from on high (John 6:33-35), should not the preacher feed his flock accordingly? If believers are 'complete in him' should we not labour to show them the Christ in whom all fullness dwells (Colossians 2:10; 1:19)? Of course we should. For he is before all things ... the head of the body, the church, the firstborn from the dead, that in all things he may have the pre-eminence' (Colossians 1:17-19). It would be a strange thing if God intended his Son to have pre-eminence in everything except our preaching!

Seeing the Father

There is another possible objection — an issue that genuinely troubles some preachers. If we preach Christ exclusively, are we not in danger of neglecting the Father — the first Person of the Godhead? This may be why many sermons refer to 'God' frequently but make little mention of Christ. For example, it is possible to preach on the glory of God from an Old Testament passages like Exodus 3:6 (the burning bush) or 33:18-23 (Moses beseeching God to show him his glory) without reference to Christ.

But we should remember that under the new covenant we behold 'the glory of God in the face of Jesus Christ' — who reveals the fullness of God's 'grace and truth' (2 Corinthians 4:6; John 1:14). By all means let us expound these Old Testament manifestations of God's glory. But let us do so by relating them to Christ, remembering that they were only shadows and precursors of 'the glory that excels' — the glory of God's beloved Son (2 Corinthians 3:10). For Christ is 'the brightness of God's glory and the express image of his person' (Hebrews 1:3). Hebrews also reminds us that we no longer come to Mount Sinai 'but... to Mount Zion and to the city of the living God' (Hebrews 12:18-24). The true glory of the living God is revealed only in Christ for 'no man has seen God at any time. The only-begotten Son, who is in the bosom of the Father, he has declared him' (John 1:18).

What shall we conclude, therefore? 'He who does not honour the Son, does not honour the Father who sent him' (John 5:23). He who has seen Christ has seen the Father (John 14:9). It is not possible, therefore, to honour Christ at the expense of honouring the Father. Rather, we exalt the Father in the same measure as we exalt his Son.

9. Preaching Christ from the Old Testament

'Then Paul ... reasoned with them from the Scriptures, explaining and demonstrating that the Christ had to suffer and rise again from the dead, and saying, "This Jesus whom I preach to you is the Christ"' (Acts 17:2-3).

Preachers seldom have difficulty preaching from the Old Testament — but preaching *Christ* from the Old Testament can be a different matter. Nevertheless this is exactly what Paul did when he arrived in Thessalonica, as the verse printed above makes clear. Of course, the OT contains many passages that are explicitly 'messianic' — that is, they make unmistakable reference to the coming Christ. Isaiah 53 is probably the best-known example, but there are many others. No one has a problem preaching Christ from such OT scriptures.

The difficulty lies in achieving a consistent and general Christological interpretation of the OT — one in which all OT Scripture is viewed as a testimony to Christ and interpreted accordingly. There are two issues. Firstly, and fundamentally, ought we be to looking for such an interpretation anyway? Secondly, if we should, how can we in practice find Christ 'in all the Scriptures'?

Icebergs or islands?

In this chapter we deal with the first of these questions. An analogy might help us address it. Consider an iceberg floating in the ocean. It is a thing of beauty but it floats freely, having no root in its watery environment. It is incidental, isolated and without enduring significance. By contrast, an island is a visible manifestation of the ocean's hidden geography — perhaps betraying the existence of an extinct volcano. It is an integral part of the ocean floor, even though that floor is mostly concealed until we take trouble to explore the depths.

Similarly, the messianic passages may be 'icebergs', beautiful in themselves but incidental, having no root in OT Scripture — dis-

connected oddities that in no way reflect the intrinsic nature of those Scriptures. On the other hand, these passages may be 'islands' — visible outcrops of a pro-found hidden reality that underpins the OT Scriptures from

Iceberg or island?

Genesis to Malachi. This, I believe, is the view of the Old Testament revealed by the New. The hidden reality, of course, is Christ. Let us consider what evidence there is to support this contention.

The evidence

Firstly, the NT epistles contain several statements which assert that the purpose of all OT Scripture is to instruct and edify new-covenant believers. Furthermore, in each case this asser-tion has a bearing on the OT's testimony to Christ. In effect they say, 'the OT was written for our benefit, and that benefit resides in Christ'.

One example is Romans 15:1-4. This passage begins with a simple moral injunction — 'we who are strong ought to bear with ... the weak, and not to please ourselves'. But Paul does not leave it there. Such moral behaviour, he insists, flows from Christ's example — 'For even Christ did not please himself, but as it is written [Psalm 69:9], "The reproaches of those who reproached you fell on me".' He continues: 'For whatsoever things were written beforehand were written for our learning, that we through the patience and comfort of the Scriptures might have hope ...' The Greek word rendered 'whatsoever things' is emphatic, implying 'everything'.

This tells us not only that the obscure citation from Psalm 69 refers to Christ but also that *all* OT Scripture was written specifically for our benefit. This benefit, says Paul, comes to us in the form of learning, patience, comfort and, above all, hope in Christ (there is no other hope).

Tempting Christ

A second statement is found in 1 Corinthians 10:8-12 where Paul warns: 'let us not tempt Christ as some of them also tempted and were destroyed by serpents ... Now all these things happened to them as examples, and they were written for our admonition, on whom the ends of the ages have come'. As in Romans 15, Paul says two things and links them together. Firstly, the very purpose of the OT — even its historical sections — is to instruct and admonish those who live under the new covenant ('on whom the ends of the ages have come'). But additionally, it is Christ we must not tempt — meaning that these Scriptures admonish us not just in general terms but in regard to our relationship with Christ. He himself tells us that 'the serpent in the wilderness' prefigured his crucifixion (John 3:14).

A third statement is found in 1 Corinthians 9:9 — 'For it is written in the law of Moses, "You shall not muzzle an ox while it treads out the grain". Is it oxen God is concerned about? Or does he say it altogether for our sakes? For our sakes no doubt this is written, that he who ploughs should plough in hope ...'

Read on and you will see that the 'ploughing' here is the work of the gospel. Once again, then, we find twin assertions — OT Scripture was written for our benefit, and that benefit relates to Christ and his gospel.

Peter concurs (1 Peter 1:8-12). He writes: 'Of this salvation [through Christ] the prophets have inquired and searched carefully, who prophesied of the grace that would come to you ... the Spirit of Christ who was in them was indicating ... beforehand the sufferings of Christ and the glories that would follow.

'To them it was revealed that, not to themselves, but to us they were ministering the things which now have been reported to you through those who have preached the gospel to you by the Holy Spirit sent from heaven'.

This could hardly be clearer. The OT prophets (a term which embraces all the OT writers) were moved by the Holy Spirit to testify of Christ's suffering and glory — and in doing so were not ministering primarily to their own generation but to those who would hear the New Testament gospel of salvation through grace.

The OT testifies of Christ

We come next to several definitive statements concerning the OT's testimony to Christ. The first is found in John 5:39 where Jesus tells the Jews: 'You search the Scriptures, for in them you think you have eternal life: and these are they which testify of me'. This is not a 'throw-away' statement, but part of an extended argument. For Jesus continues: 'if you believed Moses, you would believe me; for *he wrote about me*. But if you do not believe *his writings*, how will you believe my words?' (John 5:46-47).

Notice the choice of words. Christ does not simply say, '[the Scriptures] testify of me', which could mean that they did so incidentally. Rather he says, 'These are they which testify' — implying that the very purpose of the OT is to testify of him. Again, he states unambiguously that it is Moses' writings (that is, the whole Pentateuch) that bear witness to the Christ, not just occasional references therein. This is significant since there is a common tendency today to preach on such subjects as creation, the patriarchs, and the law of Moses, in a manner that neglects Christ. Yet according to Jesus, Moses was writing about him throughout the first five books of the Bible.

A second significant passage is Luke 24:25-27, the familiar Emmaus Road story. The risen Christ chides his shattered disciples: 'O foolish ones, and slow of heart to believe in *all* that the prophets have spoken! ... and beginning at Moses and *all* the prophets, he expounded to them in *all* the Scriptures the things concerning himself'. Note the threefold use of 'all'. Luke is clearly concerned that we should understand the comprehensive nature of Jesus' claims — namely, that all OT Scripture, not just some of it, is prophetical of Christ.

'Moses and the prophets' was shorthand for the whole Old Testament — and Jesus tells us elsewhere that he came to fulfil every 'jot and tittle' of those Scriptures (Matthew 5:17-18). If Christ is their fulfilment, they must necessarily point to him.

Wise for salvation

Our final 'proof text' is 2 Timothy 3:15-17 — 'From childhood you have known the Holy Scriptures, which are able to make you wise for salvation through faith which is in Christ Jesus. All Scripture is given by inspiration of God, and is profitable for doctrine, for reproof, for correction, for instruction in righteousness, that the man of God may be complete, thoroughly equipped for every good work'.

We often quote these words when speaking of the nature and use of Scripture — that it is inspired (literally 'God-breathed') and instructive. But we easily overlook the statement that leads Paul to describe the Old Testament in this way. What is that statement? That these OT Scriptures enlighten us regarding salvation by faith in Christ! Again Paul refers comprehensively to OT Scripture as that which reveals Christ in saving power. It is in this Christological context that the apostle further commends the Old Testament as a source-book for instruction and good works.

These Scriptures compel me to believe that the Old Testament in its entirety testifies of Christ and was written specifically for the benefit of New Testament believers — and all who desire to become 'wise for salvation' in him. The 'messianic passages' in OT Scripture are 'islands' not 'icebergs', revealing the underlying, all-embracing Christology of the Old Testament.

10. New Testament
Practice (1)

*'For [Apollos] vigorously refuted the Jews publicly,
showing from the Scriptures that Jesus is the Christ'*
(Acts 18:28).

In the last chapter we began to consider the subject 'Preaching Christ from the Old Testament'. I asked two questions — firstly, should we always seek to present Christ when preaching from the Old Testament, whatever the passage in view, and secondly, how may we do so in practice?

I answered the first of these questions in the affirmative. Among the most telling of the NT Scriptures supporting this view is 1 Peter 1:10-11 — the Old Testament writers themselves 'inquired and searched diligently, who prophesied of the grace that would come to you, searching what ... the Spirit of Christ who was in them was indicating when he testified beforehand of the sufferings of Christ and the glories that would follow'.

Having confidence, therefore, that the whole Old Testament does indeed testify of Christ, we now turn to the second question — how may we find Christ in the OT writings that we might preach him from them? This enquiry will occupy the remaining chapters in this booklet.

Reasoning from the Scriptures

All would agree, I imagine, that we should be guided in this matter by New Testament practice. The only 'Bible' available to most of the NT writers and preachers was the Old Testament. What better instructor could we have, therefore, than the New Testament if we want to preach Christ from the Old! New Testament practice in this matter is exemplified by two statement in Acts. Firstly, when Paul arrived in Thessalonica and went to the synagogue, he 'reasoned with them from the [OT] Scriptures, explaining and demonstrating that the Christ had to suffer and rise again from the dead, and saying, "This Jesus whom I preach to you is the Christ"' (17:2-3). Secondly: '[Apollos] vigorously refuted the Jews publicly, showing from the Scriptures that Jesus is the Christ' (18:28).

But exactly how did the New Testament writers and preachers 'find' Christ in all the Scriptures? They did so at three levels — in direct references to the Messiah, in types and pictures, and in what I will call 'obscure references'.

Direct references

Firstly and most clearly, they found Old Testament references that speak plainly of the Messiah and his kingdom. The many prophecies of Christ's coming are obvious examples, often re-flected in the refrain 'That it might be fulfilled ...'. These or similar words are found no fewer than 16 times in Matthew's Gospel, beginning with Matthew 1:22-23 — 'So all this was done that it might be fulfilled which was spoken by the Lord through the prophet, saying: "Behold, a virgin shall be with child, and shall bring forth a son, and they shall call his name Emmanuel", which being interpreted is, God with us'. Likewise in Luke 4:21 Jesus declares concerning himself, 'Today this Scripture is fulfilled in your hearing' (he was referring to Isaiah 61:1-2). Similar state-ments occur throughout the Gospels, Acts and Revelation.

Another kind of direct reference is found where the NT takes up an OT passage concerning Jehovah (or JAHWE) and applies it — without any reticence or apology — to Christ. An outstanding example is God's statement in Isaiah 45:23 — 'I have sworn by myself; the word has gone out of my mouth in righteousness and shall not return, that to me every knee shall bow, every tongue shall take an oath'.

Paul applies this Scripture to Christ, not once but twice — in Romans 14:10-11 and Philippians 2:9-11: 'God also has highly exalted him and given him the name which is above every name, that at the name of Jesus every knee should bow and every tongue confess that Jesus Christ is Lord, to the glory of God the Father'. A further example is John 12:37-41 which tells us that Isaiah's temple vision was of Christ enthroned (Isaiah 6:10).

Types and pictures

At the second level, the New Testament writers and teachers discovered Christ in Old Testament types and pictures. Buck's Theological Dictionary defines a type as 'an impression, image, or representation of some model, which is termed the antitype'. Biblical antitypes include Christ himself, the death of Christ, the church and kingdom of Christ, salvation, and other spiritual realities. A type can also be defined as something that is self-evidently symbolic. For example, the mercy seat symbolised Christ crucified, both as the cause and locus of God's mercy to sinners. Needless to say, the Old Testament teems with such types and pictures which (as we saw in the last chapter) were specifically given to provide insight, instruction and illumination in relation to their new-covenant antitypes. This is why they constitute such a rich store of material for Christ-centred preaching today.

Such types and pictures include: animal sacrifices representing Christ's atoning work (e.g. 'Christ, our Passover, was sacrificed for us'); OT kings, priests and warriors representing Christ's kingdom, priestly intercession and spiritual conquests;

Moses representing Christ's headship; the tabernacle representing Christ's ministry; the Shekinah representing Christ's glory;
the rock representing Christ in his eternal power; Israel representing Christ's people; the promised land representing salvation;
and the temple representing Christ's church.

Obscure references

The third level at which the New Testament writers found Christ
in the Old is less clear-cut but just as real. There are places in the
New Testament where Old Testament texts are applied to Christ
which would otherwise seem to have no Christological significance. One example is Galatians 3:16, where Paul interprets the
promise made to Abraham's 'seed' as referring to
Christ in person, when we would more naturally
understand it to mean Abraham's descendants
generally. Again, in Galatians 4:21-31, he uses the
story of Sarah and Hagar as a profound allegory
concerning the old and new covenants.

Another case is Isaiah 8:16-18: 'Bind up the
testimony. Seal the law among my disciples ... I
will hope in [the Lord]. Here am I and the children whom the
Lord has given me!' Hebrews 2:12-14 apply these words to Christ,
even though their messianic import is far from clear in the OT
text. The same is true of other Scriptures cited in Hebrews, such
as Psalm 8:4-6 (Hebrews 2:6-9) and Habakkuk 2:3-4 (Hebrews
10:36-39).

Peter takes up Proverbs 26:11 — 'a dog returns to his own
vomit' — and applies it to those who apostasize from Christ. And
who would have recognised Christ and his gospel in the personi-
fied 'wisdom' of Proverbs 8 unless Paul had written, 'Christ [is]
the power of God and the wisdom of God' (1 Corinthians 1:24)?
So we could continue.

Clearly, this 'obscure' category is broad, embracing everything from a single proverb to a lengthy narrative like the story of Joseph — where there is an 'obscure' but discernible pattern of Christ's death and resurrection. We probably need to include here also the 'theophanies' (appearances of God) where the pre-incarnate Christ appeared to Old Testament believers in human form (e.g. Joshua 5:13-15; Daniel 3:24-25).

A problem

A problem that confronts us with 'obscure texts' is that the NT authors wrote under the guidance and inspiration of the Holy Spirit — ensuring that their interpretations were reliable. But if we ourselves impose Christological interpretations on 'obscure' OT texts that are not specifically mentioned in the NT, we have no such guarantee. This is true, and we need to be cautious in approaching such texts. However, we must also remember that we have a general remit to interpret the OT in a Christological manner, as we saw in the previous chapter. It is important to keep this balance in mind.

A classic example is the centuries-old debate over the interpretation of the Song of Solomon. Is it just a beautiful and instructive love story? Or is it an allegory concerning Christ and his church? I believe it speaks of Christ and the church. Why? Because the church is pictured in several NT scriptures as the bride of Christ, who is the bridegroom. From this new-covenant perspective the Song of Solomon makes most sense if understood in this way. This is instructive. We need to justify our interpretation of an OT text in terms of overall NT teaching. But provided we can do so, we should not hesitate to expound it in a Christological manner.

Conclusion

As a preliminary to preaching Christ from the Old Testament we need to discover Christ therein. How may we do so? By following the practice of the New Testament writers and preachers, who for the most part had no Scriptures except the Old Testament.

Of course, they were themselves in the process of receiving fresh revelation (Ephesians 3:5) which is no longer the case with us. But they were careful to demonstrate that this new revelation was wholly consistent with the Old Testament, and commended those like the Bereans who 'received the word [the NT gospel] with all readiness and searched the [OT] Scriptures daily to find out whether these things were so' (Acts 17:11). At each level, therefore, we should adopt a New Testament perspective and follow New Testament practice as we seek to find Christ in the Old Testament — in direct references, typology and even obscure texts.

11. NEW TESTAMENT PRACTICE (2)

'Then Philip opened his mouth and beginning at this Scripture preached Jesus to him' (Acts 8:35)

In the last chapter we identified three ways in which New Testament writers and preachers 'found' Christ in the Old Testament — in direct Messianic references, in types and pictures, and in what I called 'obscure references'. Let us now illustrate this approach from the preaching in Acts.

Arriving at Christ

We begin with the verse that heads this page. Philip, sent by the Spirit to the Gaza road, meets an Ethiopian eunuch 'of great authority' returning from Jerusalem in his chariot. The man is reading Isaiah 53:7-8 — 'He was led as a sheep to the slaughter'. He asks Philip, 'Of whom does the prophet say this?'

In reply, Philip 'opened his mouth and beginning at this Scripture preached Jesus to him'. The actual sermon is not recorded, of course, but enough is said to demonstrate Philip's method.

Here was a Messianic passage in which, however, Christ is identified only as the 'righteous servant' of the Lord who 'shall justify many'. So while Philip could *begin* at this Scripture he could not finish there! It was necessary for him to link the messianic promise to the One who had now come in the flesh — Jesus of Nazareth. Clearly, the link was not just with Jesus as a man. Philip had to explain in what sense Jesus was 'righteous' — and to what effect. He would have told the Ethiopian how Jesus had secured the justification of many by his death and resurrection (Romans 4:25). He must even have explained the significance of baptism, for otherwise the man would not have asked to be baptised!

We see here the basic elements of New Testament method. The OT prophecy was used as a starting point — a spring-board — from which to preach specifically about Jesus of Nazareth and his atoning work. The messianic promise was spelled out, leaving no room for misunderstanding what it meant — both objectively and for the Ethiopian personally. Regardless of where we start, we must arrive at 'Jesus Christ and him crucified'.

Joel and Jesus

Our second example is also a case of 'direct reference' — Peter's sermon on the day of Pentecost (Acts 2:14-39). Peter begins with an explanation. The amazing things happening before their eyes were, he said, the fulfilment of OT prophecy ('This is what was spoken by the prophet ...'). In this way he links his audience's present and personal experience to Scripture. This is important. In preaching Christ from the Old Testament we need to relate the Scriptures to our hearers' own circumstances. Peter wasn't giving a history lesson and neither should we!

Even more important is the fact that he immediately links Joel's prophecy to Jesus Christ. Had Joel predicted 'wonders' and 'signs' from God? Then also 'Jesus [was] a man attested by God to you by miracles, wonders and signs ...' In other words, Peter draws from the prophecy not just an explanation of some puzzling events but a testimony to the deity and power of Christ.

Having introduced Christ as the man 'attested by God', Peter moves swiftly to the crucifixion — which he attributes firstly to the sovereign, redeeming purpose of God and only secondly to the lawlessness of the Jews. The death of Christ is central to the plan of salvation, and thus to New Testament preaching (1 Corinthians 2:2).

As proof of all this, continues Peter, God has raised Jesus from the dead. He then launches into another OT passage, namely Psalm 16:8-11, actually putting David's words into the mouth of Christ. Peter justifies 'finding Christ' in the psalm by pointing out that the words could not possibly apply to David himself. Rather, he says, David 'foreseeing ... the resurrection of the Christ' spoke of 'this Jesus [whom] God raised up'.

Next, citing a third Scripture (Psalm 110:1), Peter speaks of Christ's victorious exaltation to the throne of God — he is both Lord and King (Acts 2:30-31). Finally, returning to Joel, Peter presents the outpouring of God's Spirit as the gift of Christ — fulfilling the ancient promise and opening the way of salvation to all peoples.

The importance of links

We can learn much from the way Peter uses the Old Testament in preaching Christ. He employs three apparently unrelated OT passages like steps on a ladder. He quotes one Scripture, draws out its Messianic content, and then builds on it by linking it to Jesus of Nazareth — before repeating the process with a second Scripture and then a third.

Each new Scripture moves his hearers on — from God's attestation of a man, to Christ's atoning death, to his vindicating resurrection, to his enthronement in heaven, and finally (reverting to Joel) to the promise of salvation through the gift of the Spirit. An essential part of this process is the way Peter links each OT passage firmly to Jesus Christ — that is, to New Testament revelation. Such linkages are vital, for OT passages as they stand, seldom display the fullness of the new-covenant in Christ — they require the added light of the New Testament if they are to illuminate our hearts and minds concerning him.

So in our own preaching we should always link our chosen

OT verses to NT Scriptures — making explicit what might otherwise remain obscure. Then, in turn, the OT passage will help to fill out and enrich the NT truth that it foreshadows. An excellent example is the way the death of Christ fulfils the animal sacrifices of the Old Testament, while the animal sacrifices prepare us to understand the forensic and substitutionary nature of Christ's death as an atonement for sin.

Types and pictures

The second way that the sermons in *Three texts as a ladder ...*
Acts 'find Christ' in the OT is in types and pictures. Such usage is actually less frequent in Acts than in Jesus' own sermons — for example, the serpent in the wilderness, the sign of the prophet Jonah, the temple rebuilt in three days, and so on. The NT epistles (especially Hebrews) also make extensive use of OT typology.

Nevertheless, there are examples in the messages in Acts. In Acts 4:5-12, Peter defends himself before the rulers and elders by citing Psalm 118:22 — 'This is the stone which was rejected by you builders, which has become the chief corner stone'. This quotation actually contains three 'types'. Firstly, Christ typified as the 'chief corner stone' of God's spiritual temple. Secondly, the temple itself (implied) is used to picture the church of Christ. Thirdly, the Jews, are typified as the 'builders' — who should have constructed God's kingdom on earth but failed miserably to do so.

But the most important thing is the way Peter uses this typology to underline the uniqueness and supremacy of Christ. Having quoted the psalm he continues, 'nor is there salvation in any other, for there is no other name under heaven given among men by which we must be saved' (Acts 4:12).

David's tabernacle

A second example is found in James' address to the Council of Jerusalem (Acts 15:13-21). Referring to the conversion of the Gentiles, he quotes Amos 9:11-12 — 'After this I will return and will rebuild the tabernacle of David which has fallen down ... so that the rest of mankind may seek the Lord'.

It matters little whether the 'tabernacle of David' refers to the actual tabernacle which disappeared from the OT record following David's death, or whether it refers to David's 'house' or dynasty. Either way, it is a picture of Christ who 'tabernacled' among us and was 'raised up to sit on David's throne' — and who draws to himself 'the rest of mankind', Gentiles as well as Jews. The typology is crucial to James' case. At the Council of Jerusalem, the whole future of the Christian church was at stake. Were believing Gentiles indeed fellow heirs of Abraham along with believing Jews? Was Christianity simply an extension of the law of Moses, or had a new covenant been inaugurated? By interpreting 'the tabernacle of David' as a reference to Christ, and applying the type powerfully to the dispute in hand, James guides the Council firmly to a right conclusion — and opens wide the door of faith to all the peoples of the earth.

In the next chapter we shall consider the use in Acts of 'obscure references' — that is, OT Scriptures from which Christ is preached but which are not self-evidently either Messianic predictions or types and pictures.

12. STEPHEN'S SERMON

'They also set up false witnesses who said ...
"We have heard him say that this Jesus of Nazareth will ...
change the customs which Moses delivered to us"'
(Acts 6:13-14)

We have seen how New Testament preachers 'found' Christ in the Old Testament in Messianic prophecies and types. But they also found him in what I called 'obscure references' — OT texts which at first sight have nothing to do with Christ. Consider now this aspect of New Testament practice, using Stephen's sermon in Acts 7 as our example.

History lesson?

From the charges brought against Stephen (see opening text) it is clear enough that he was intent on preaching Christ. But his long sermon in Acts 7:1-53 makes no mention of 'Jesus' or 'the Christ' — it seems to be a simple history lesson! To be fair, he does refer briefly to Christ as the 'prophet like Moses' (v.37) and 'the Just One' (v.52). It was the latter statement, in fact, that triggered the wrath of his persecutors. But for the most part he just rehearses Old Testament history with no obvious application to Christ. Was Stephen really preaching Christ, then? Yes — and he was doing so throughout the sermon, in spite of appearances.

Stephen's use of history to preach Christ is specially significant, because the historical sections of the Old Testament often seem devoid of Christological content. The Law overflows with types and pictures of Christ. The Psalms are replete with Messianic hope. The prophets also testify plainly of the One who was to come. But where is Christ in the historical narratives of the Old Testament?

A principle of interpretation

At first sight these histories are a featureless desert for the would-be preacher of Christ. But Stephen knew better. He understood a principle that Paul later spells out. Writing of Israel's troubled history in the wilderness, Paul tells the equally troubled church at Corinth: 'Now all these things happened to them as examples, and they were written for our admonition on whom the ends of the ages have come' (1 Corinthians 10:11).

'The things that happened' constitute the history of Israel. Paul is telling us that this arcane and ancient narrative was set down under the Holy Spirit's guidance for our instruction and benefit — those to whom Christ would one day be proclaimed. The same truth is taught in Hebrews 3:5, which says, 'Moses indeed was faithful in all his house as a servant, for a testimony of those things that would be spoken afterwards [that is, in the gospel era]'. See also Romans 15:4. Let us, then, see this principle at work in Stephen's message to the Jewish Council.

Christ in the promise

Stephen begins by laying a foundation, namely, the promise God made to Abraham and sealed by the 'covenant of circumcision' (vv. 5-8). Stephen is reminding them that the essence of Jewish nationhood lay in their being heirs of this promise. As we know, God's promise to Abraham culminates in the 'seed' through whom all the nations of the earth would be blessed — which seed is Christ (Galatians 3:16).

Stephen's audience were well versed in the Scriptures and should have understood the Messianic implications of the promise. Whether or not they did so, they were given clear notice that this sermon concerned the fulfilment of the promise in the coming Christ. Logically, at this point Stephen introduces the dominant theme of his sermon — the envy and rejection meted out to God's chosen ones by their Jewish brethren throughout history. This rejection, of course, foreshadowed and culminated in their rejection of the promised Christ.

Christ and Joseph

featureless desert or fruitful field?

This emerges first in verse 9, where Stephen relates how Joseph was envied and rejected by his brethren. However, 'God was with him and delivered him out of all his troubles' (vv. 9-10). This is the balancing truth — those whom the Jews reject are nevertheless raised up by God. Jesus of Nazareth is already clearly in view! Furthermore, not only was Joseph elevated to high office in Egypt, but he was received by his brethren (and former enemies) as one who had returned from the dead. And having been made known to them, Joseph became their saviour from famine and death (vv. 13-14). Again, the Messianic implications may have been lost on Stephen's audience, but they were clearly present in the preacher's mind, as we shall see.

Next, Stephen reminds them how God's words to Abraham concerning Israel's enslavement and deliverance from Egypt were precisely fulfilled (compare vv. 6-7 with vv. 17-19). If that were so, would not his promise concerning the 'seed' also be fulfilled?

Christ and Moses

Stephen now launches into the longest section of his sermon — that which features the history of Israel under Moses (vv. 20ff). He begins by emphasising the sad condition of Israel in Egypt. He extols Moses as the child 'well-pleasing to God' and as one full of wisdom. Moses was also 'mighty in words and deed', a phrase used by the early disciples to describe Jesus — 'a prophet mighty in deed and word before God and all the people' (Luke 24:19). But Stephen's main point about Moses was that, like Joseph before him, he was rejected by his brethren — 'he supposed that his brethren would have understand that God would deliver them by his hand, but they did not understand' (v.25). The preacher underscores his point. 'This Moses whom they rejected ... is the one God sent to be a ruler and a deliverer' (v.35).

I am sure that by this stage the hearers were beginning to 'get the message'. Stephen was not simply rehearsing history but was demonstrating that the Jews had consistently rejected those whom God sent historically to save them. Nevertheless, through the sovereign mercy of God, the saviours they rejected were raised up to save them, notwithstanding their sin (v.36)! So aptly do they prefigure Christ.

Christ and the law

Not only did Israel reject God's 'saviours' — they also rejected his law. Moses 'received the living oracles to give to us, whom our fathers would not obey, but rejected. And in their hearts they turned back to Egypt ...' (v.39). Yet, amazingly, the Lord did not utterly reject them. By grace he brought them into the promised land under Joshua, himself a 'saviour' and a notable type of Christ (v.45). Furthermore, they were accompanied into the land by the tabernacle, an evident token of God's presence among them. But they did not understand the token, nor the symbolism of the temple that succeeded it. They did not understand that 'the Most High does not dwell in temples made with hands' (v.48). Thus they again rejected precious truth — the truth that One who had 'tabernacled' among them was the true temple. Him they had destroyed only to see him raised again in three days (John 2:19).

Christ and the prophets

Stephens's final denouncement cites the Jews' rejection of the prophets, 'who foretold the coming of the Just One' (v.52). This culminated in their ultimate crime — the rejection, betrayal and murder of the very Deliverer of whom the prophets spoke (v.52).

We do not know what more Stephen intended to say. It is almost certain that, like Peter, he would have gone on to declare that in spite of their wickedness, God had raised Jesus from the dead and made him 'both Lord and Christ'. In his name they could receive 'the remission of sins' and 'the gift of the Holy Spirit' (Acts 2:36-38). That was, after all, the repeated message of his sermon — that God raises up saviours to deliver those who once rejected them. Stephen would have told them so. But they killed him before he could.

At first sight, then, Stephen's sermon was nothing but Jewish history. But looking deeper we see how he found in the historical narrative a pattern that prefigured Christ with glorious clarity. According to that pattern, God's people were again and again distressed and ready to perish — whether from hunger in Canaan, enslavement in Egypt, or by languishing in the wilderness. Each time God sends them a saviour, but they reject him and his message. They also reject the law-givers and prophets who proclaim salvation to those with eyes to see it.

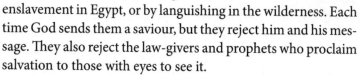

Each time, however, God rejects rejection! He raises up the rejected one, exalting him to a place of authority from which he proceeds to save the very people who rebelled against him. In short, Stephen uses Jewish history to prefigure and proclaim

Christ — rejected, crucified, resurrected, and 'exalted to [God's] right hand to be a Prince and a Saviour, to give repentance to Israel and the forgiveness of sins' (Acts 5:31).

If Stephen can preach Christ from Jewish history, so can we — and from every other portion of God word in the Old Testament, even if at first it seems obscure. In doing so we have the full support of New Testament practice.

13. CHRIST IN ALL THE SCRIPTURES

*'Whatsoever things were written beforehand were written
for our learning, that we through
the patience and comfort
of the Scriptures might have hope'
(Romans 15:4).*

In concluding this booklet, I want to outline two sermons from Old Testament passages that, at first sight, are 'obscure' as regards their Christological content. May they encourage us all to find 'Christ in all the Scriptures'.

Our first sermon is based on Joshua 5 and could be entitled, 'The reproach of Egypt removed' (5:9). Under Joshua's leadership the Israelites had crossed the Jordan, its angry flood-waters held at bay by the Ark of the Covenant which pictures Christ. They had escaped the wilderness of unbelief and had been translated into Canaan — the promised land which they must now possess and which pictures salvation rather than heaven (Hebrews 4:6-10; Colossians 1:12-14). But their progress is abruptly halted. Before they can proceed, all the males must be circumcised (5:2-3). Why was this important? Consider the answer under three headings — the sign of the covenant; the sins of the flesh; and the sufficiency of Christ.

The sign of the covenant

God gave circumcision as the sign and seal of his covenant with Abraham (Genesis 17:7-14; Romans 4:11). The covenant in question was not that of Sinai but the covenant of promise — which has its ultimate fulfilment in Christ (Galatians 3:15-18). But it also had an historical fulfilment in the occupation of the land of Canaan (Genesis 17:8).

To whom would God give the promised land? Only to the heirs of the promise — who bore the sign of the covenant. But the nation that entered Canaan with Joshua lacked that sign. The ritual of circumcision has been suspended during their 40 years in the wilderness, underlining God's displeasure at their unbelief (5:5-6; compare Genesis 17:14). Before they could possess the land, therefore, they must be 're-admitted' to the covenant of promise by the restoration of its sign. What can we learn from this?

The covenant of promise is fulfilled in the new covenant in Christ; the land pictures salvation; and physical circumcision prefigures the circumcision of the heart — 'In Christ Jesus neither circumcision nor uncircumcision avails anything, but a new creation' (Galatians 6:15). We see, therefore, that only the true heirs of Abraham — who share his faith, and (being born again) are new creations in Christ — are qualified to possess the land of salvation (Galatians 3:9, 29).

The reproach of Egypt (5:9) was slavery, but it was not removed when Israel escaped from Pharaoh. Why not? Because Israel remained in bondage to unbelief. Only now, as they came afresh under the covenant of promise, was that reproach finally removed. So must we find refuge under the 'new covenant in [Jesus'] blood' (1 Corinthians 11:25) if we are to inherit the kingdom of heaven.

The sins of the flesh

Concerning the circumcision of the heart, Paul writes: 'In him you were circumcised with the circumcision made without hands, by putting off the body of the sins of the flesh, by the circumcision of Christ' (Colossians 2:11). Under the new covenant, physical circumcision is meaningless, but it remains a picture of the new creation that has been wrought in Christ. Moses, foresaw this clearly: 'The Lord God will bring you [back] to the land which your fathers possessed, and you shall possess it ... and the Lord your God will circumcise your hearts ... to love the Lord your God with all your heart and with all your soul, that you may live' (Deuteronomy 30:5-6).

Only those who have received this spiritual circumcision are qualified to possess the land and its riches — the unsearchable riches of Christ. They have 'put off the old man with his deeds and have put on the new man who is renewed in knowledge according to the image of him who created him' (Colossians 3:9-10). They have laid aside the '[evil] desires of the flesh

Model of the second temple

and of the mind' and have become God's workmanship, 'created in Christ Jesus for good works, which God prepared beforehand that we should walk in them' (Ephesians 2:3, 10).

The sufficiency of Christ

Paul's words about spiritual circumcision are part of an extended argument. The preceding verses state: 'In [Christ] dwells all the fullness of the Godhead bodily, and you are complete in him, who is the head of all principality and power' (Colossians 2:9-10). The Colossians were being drawn away from a Christ-centred faith towards Judaistic and Gnostic corruptions of the gospel. Their false teachers were urging them to observe Jewish customs and seek esoteric wisdom. Paul's message in this context is that believers are 'complete' in Christ, who is head over all things and the substance of all true religion (2:17-19). Having been 'circumcised' by Christ — cleansed from sin and raised from spiritual death (2:13-14) — they needed no other provision. Those who are circumcised in heart are complete in Christ. He is all they need for time and for eternity.

To beautify the Lord's house

Our second outline sermon is based on Ezra 7:11-28, which records King Artaxerxes' commission to Ezra to return from Babylon to Jerusalem to revive temple worship and refurbish the temple itself. While the Joshua example is clearly tied to an explicit symbol, this second example reflects an implicit pattern.

A single verse opens up the whole passage. In v.27 we read Ezra's response to the gracious provisions the king had made: 'Blessed be the Lord God of our fathers, who has put such a thing as this in the king's heart, to beautify the house of the Lord which is at Jerusalem'. The passage, then, is all about beautifying God's house — which typifies the church of Jesus Christ (Ephesians 2:19-22; Hebrews 3:6; 1 Peter 2:5-10).

The king's problem

Although completely rebuilt only 70 years earlier, the temple had fallen on hard times. Concerned that all was not well — and fearing divine wrath if God's name was dishonoured through negligence (7:23) — Artaxerxes sent Ezra to Jerusalem to teach the law and set in order the worship of 'the God of heaven' (7:14). Ezra's later chapters focus on the failings he found, particularly compromise with the world through intermarriage with idol worshippers (Ezra 9:1-15). How clear a picture this is of the

professing church today! Even within Evangelical churches we
see much that dishonours God through compromise and ac-
commodation with the world. Our passage therefore addresses
a current and topical need.

The king's purpose

Artaxerxes' purpose was not just to prop
up an ailing religion — it was to beautify
the temple. He sought not just its survival
but its transformation. Similarly, God's purpose (and our desire) is to see the church
of Christ in our own day changed out of
all recognition. But what can be done to
'beautify' the church of Christ? Answers
are given here in the letter of Artaxerxes,
'king of kings' (7:12). So we shall find answers in the book of
God which brings us to the ultimate King of kings and Lord of
lords, even Jesus Christ (Revelation 19:16). It is Christ's purpose
to present to himself a glorious church, without wrinkle and
without spot (Ephesians 5:27).

The king's perception

Artaxerxes sends to Jerusalem neither a diplomat nor a figure-
head but a humble priest. Herein we see the kings perception,
for Ezra was 'expert in the words of the commandments of the
Lord and of his statutes to Israel' — he was 'a scribe of the law
of the God of heaven' (7:11-12).

If the church is to be beautified it must be taught the Word
of God — the living law and message of a sovereign God. Neglect
the ministry of that Word and the church will decline. To minister the Word aright, however, we must minister Christ, for the

Scriptures testify of him (John 5:39). A biblical, Christ-centred ministry will enliven and beautify the church.

The king's power

Ezra was sent not only by the king but also by his 'seven counsellors' (7:14). We see here a reference to the Holy Spirit (Zechariah 3:9; 4:10; Revelation 1:4). The Word alone will not revive God's people and beautify the church, but the Word and the Spirit together will do so. When Paul preached 'Christ and him crucified', his preaching was 'in demonstration of the Spirit and of power' (1 Corinthians 2:2-5). It is the Spirit's work to reveal and glorify Christ (John 16:13-15). The Spirit also helps our infirmities as we seek to intercede with God, and searches the deep things of God that we might have the mind of Christ (Romans 8:26-27; 1 Corinthians 2:10-16).

The king's provision

Finally, out of 'the king's treasury' Artaxerxes provided richly for Ezra's every need (7:20). The silver and gold of Babylon was put at his disposal, along with the free-will offerings of God's people (7:15-16). These riches were not to be squandered but used in the worship and service of God (7:17-18). So also God supplies the needs of his work and of his people out of 'his riches in glory by Christ Jesus' (Philippians 4:19). Let us avail ourselves of that supply!

Space forbids further exploration of this wonderfully pregnant passage — but be aware that there is much more in this passage to reveal how God will beautify his church on earth, that she might be fit to glorify him in heaven. See if you can find it!